Hi Jim!

Happy Birthday!

Gundline

Something to remember me

by

Weltkulturerbe WIEN

World Cultural Heritage Site Vienna

Weltkulturerbe
World Heritage

Wer einen Schatz besitzt, der sollte ihn hüten. Das weiß jedes Kind. Eine ganz andere Frage ist die der Zuständigkeit. Wer soll die Schätze der Menschheit auf Dauer bewahren, die eine Menge dieser Prachtexemplare ihr Eigen nennt? Man denke nur an die Pyramiden von Gizeh, die Freiheitsstatue von New York, den Tower of London oder das Schloss von Versailles. Die Staaten, in denen sie liegen, sollten diese Verantwortung tragen. Das stellte die UNESCO als Organisation der Vereinten Nationen für Bildung, Wissenschaft, Kultur und Kommunikation 1972 klar und gründete die „Internationale Konvention für das Kultur- und Naturerbe der Menschheit". Wer sie unterzeichnet – 178 Staaten haben dies bisher getan – der hat innerhalb der Ländergrenzen liegende Baudenkmäler, Natur- sowie Kulturlandschaften ab diesem Zeitpunkt nachhaltig zu schützen. Jedes Mitgliedsland kann einen Antrag auf Aufnahme einer Welterbestätte stellen. Das Welterbekomitee (World Heritage Comittee) der UNESCO entscheidet dann, ob die jeweilige Stätte die Kriterien erfüllt, um in die Liste des Welterbes aufgenommen zu werden. 878 eingetragene Kultur- und Naturbestätten aus 145 Ländern gibt es derzeit, 679 von ihnen sind Kulturdenkmäler, 25 gehören beiden Kategorien an. Ist eine von ihnen irgendwann in der Existenz nachhaltig beeinträchtigt oder bedroht, landet sie auf der „Roten Liste" und es wird dem zugehörigen Staat aufgetragen, sie zu sichern.

He who owns an object of value should look after it. Every child knows that. The question of responsibility is another matter. Who, for example, should preserve the great treasures of humanity in the long term? After all, there are many of them. Take the pyramids of Giza, for example, the Statue of Liberty in New York, the Tower of London, or the Palace of Versailles. The states in which they are located should bear this responsibility. That was made plain in 1972 by the UNESCO, the United Nations Educational, Scientific and Cultural Organisation, which founded the International Convention Concerning the Protection of the World Cultural and Natural Heritage. The countries which sign it – 178 states have done so up to now – have to lastingly protect historical monuments and listed buildings, as well as natural and cultural landscapes within their borders. Each member nation can apply to have a World Heritage Site recognised. The UNESCO World Heritage Committee then decides whether the site in question fulfils the criteria for inclusion in the World Cultural Heritage List. There are currently 878 listed cultural and natural heritage sites in 145 countries. Of these, 679 are cultural sites and 25 belong to both categories. If the existence of one of these sites is at any time seriously impaired or endangered, it is put on the 'Red List' and the respective country is called upon to ensure its protection.

Weltkulturerbestätten: Pyramiden von Gizeh, Stonehenge, Chinesische Mauer
World Cultural Heritage sites: Pyramids of Giza, Stonehenge, Chinese Wall

Österreich ist mit acht Schätzen gesegnet:

- Das historische Zentrum von Wien
- Schloss und Park Schönbrunn in Wien
- Das historische Zentrum von Salzburg
- Die Region Hallstatt-Dachstein/ Salzkammergut
- Die Semmeringbahn
- Das historische Zentrum von Graz
- Die Kulturlandschaft Wachau
- Die Region Neusiedlersee/Fertö (Österreich und Ungarn)

Austria is fortunate to contain eight such treasures:

- The historical centre of Vienna
- Palace and Gardens of Schönbrunn (in Vienna)
- The historical centre of Salzburg
- The region Hallstatt-Dachstein/ Salzkammergut
- The Semmering Railway
- The historical centre of Graz
- The Wachau cultural landscape
- The Lake Neusiedl/Fertö region (Austria and Hungary)

Mittelalter
Middle Ages

Barock
Baroque

Gründerzeit
Wilhelminian period

Wien verfügt über zwei Weltkulturerbestätten:

Das Schloss Schönbrunn mit seiner prächtigen Parkanlage und das historische Zentrum von Wien.

Während Schönbrunn als besonders gut erhaltenes Beispiel einer barocken Residenz 1996 als Welterbestätte anerkannt wurde, erfolgte die Aufnahme des historischen Zentrums von Wien in die Welterbeliste im Jahr 2001. Die Begründung der UNESCO: Die städtischen und architektonischen Qualitäten sind ein hervorragendes Beispiel für den Wertewandel im 2. Jahrtausend nach Christus. Drei Kulturperioden sind im historischen Zentrum von Wien außergewöhnlich gut dokumentiert:

- Das Mittelalter (14. und 15. Jahrhundert)
- Die Zeit des Barock (17. und 18. Jahrhundert)
- Die Gründerzeit (Zweite Hälfte des 19. Jahrhunderts und Jahrhundertwende)

Außerdem wird die Rolle Wiens als Musikhauptstadt Europas hervorgehoben. Die Kernzone des Weltkulturerbes umfasst den 1. Bezirk von Wien und Schloss Belvedere.

Vienna has two World Cultural Heritage Sites:

Schönbrunn Palace with its magnificent park and the historical centre of Vienna.

Whereas Schönbrunn – as a particularly well-preserved example of a Baroque palace – was recognised as a World Heritage Site in 1996, the historical centre of Vienna did not become part of the World Heritage List until 2001. UNESCO's reasons for its inclusion were that the urban and architectural qualities of the site are an outstanding example for the change in values in the second millennium after Christ's birth. Three cultural epochs are extraordinarily well illustrated in the historical centre of Vienna:

- The Middle Ages (14th and 15th century)
- The Baroque period (17th and 18th century)
- The Wilhelminian period (second half of the 19th century and the turn of the century)

The UNESCO also emphasised Vienna's role as Europe's 'classical music capital'. The core area of the World Cultural Heritage Site includes the central 1st district of Vienna and Belvedere Palace.

Weltkulturerbestätte: Region Hallstatt-Dachstein / Salzkammergut
World Cultural Heritage site: Region Hallstatt-Dachstein / Salzkammergut

Ruprechtskirche

Stephansdom

Karlskirche

Oberes Belvedere

Parlament

Rathaus

Hofburg

Schloss Schönbrunn

ÖSTERREICH 55

ÖSTERREICH 55

ÖSTERREICH 55

ÖSTERREICH 55

ÖSTERREICH 55

ÖSTERREICH 55

ÖSTERREICH 55

ÖSTERREICH 55

World Cultural Heritage Site Vienna

Inhaltsverzeichnis
Table of Content

Mittelalter / Middle Ages

Barock / Baroque

Gründerzeit / Wilhelminian period

Wien im Mittelalter
Vienna in the Middle Ages

If we were to take a trip back to the time around 1200, at the site of Vienna we would find village settlements which had arisen in the area of the old Roman camp and were now melding to form a single city. It has all the features characteristic of cities in the Middle Ages – a city wall, castle, market and churches. In this case, the first buildings of the Hofburg, Hoher Markt and the Ruprechtskirche. The latter is the first church in Vienna to be historically mentioned and is situated, as would be expected, at the site of the Roman Vindobona. The lower storeys of the tower, erected around 1130, and the main nave are the oldest walls of the city still standing today. In this era churches were focal points around which marketplaces, residential buildings and fortresses were built. Other streets in today's Austrian federal capital also hark back to a rich past: Naglergasse, interestingly, is the lane where nailers and pin makers, resided. According to the Guild Code of 1378, these groups were to pursue their crafts in the lower part of the street, where they were to reside as well. They manufactured various types of nails and pins. Even today, one is able to identify the medieval layout of the city by the way in which the narrow street curves off to the right at the end.

Wagen wir die Zeitreise ins Wien um 1200. Die Dorfsiedlungen, die auf dem Gebiet des alten Römerlagers entstanden, sind allmählich zu einer Stadt zusammengewachsen. Und diese verfügt über alle Voraussetzungen, die das Wesen einer mittelalterlichen Stadt ausmachen – Stadtmauer, Burg, Markt und Kirchen, sprich die ersten Gebäude der Hofburg, den Hohen Markt und die Ruprechtskirche. Letztere ist die erste erwähnte Kirche Wiens und liegt konsequenterweise auf dem römischen Vindobona. Ihre unteren, um 1130 errichteten Turmgeschosse und das Hauptschiff sind die ältesten noch erhaltenen Mauern der Stadt. Kirchen sind zu dieser Zeit Kristallisationspunkte, um die Marktplätze, Wohnhäuser und Befestigungen errichtet werden. Geschichtsträchtig zeigen sich aber auch andere Plätzchen der heutigen Bundeshauptstadt, etwa die Naglergasse, in der die „Nadler" und „Nagler" daheim sind. Nach der Zunftordnung von 1378 führen sie im unteren Teil der Straße ihr Gewerbe aus und wohnen auch dort. Sie gehören der Gattung der Schmiede an und stellen verschiedene Nadel- und Nagelarten her. Man erkennt noch heute die mittelalterliche Struktur der Stadt an der Rechtskrümmung am Ende der Gasse.

Ruprechtskirche im romanischen Stil,
Mittelalterliche Häuser in der Naglergasse;
Romanesque Ruprechtskirche,
Medieval buildings in Naglergasse

Gassen und Plätze
Streets and squares

Eine andere Gegend, in der man noch das mittelalterliche Wien spüren kann, ist der Judenplatz. In einer eigenen Stadt innerhalb der Stadt, die 1294 erstmals erwähnt wird, leben im mittelalterlichen Wien 800 Juden: Händler, Kreditgeber und Gelehrte. Ihr Mittelpunkt ist der Judenplatz. Dieser beherbergt neben einem Spital auch eine Synagoge und eine Schule. Gleich ums Eck liegt die Kurrentgasse, in der eine besondere Berufsgruppe lebt: Kurrenten, die Steuereintreiber. Begrenzt wird die Judenstadt im Norden durch eine Kirche: Maria am Gestade. Sie liegt im Mittelalter noch direkt am Ufer der Donau. Donauschiffer können auf ihren Kähnen den hoch aufragenden Turm der Kirche schon von weitem erkennen. Gleich daneben fließt der Ottakringer Bach, den die Tuchmacher und Tuchfärber für ihre Arbeit verwenden und der später umgeleitet wird. Das ehemalige Bachbett wird jedoch nie ganz aufgeschüttet und ist heute noch erkennbar, als „Tiefer Graben". Mittelalterliches Flair kann man heute auch noch in der Gegend rund um die Schönlaterngasse erleben. Die schmalen, verwinkelten Gässchen atmen den Geist dieser Zeit.

Judenplatz is another square which today still exudes Vienna's medieval flavour. In their own city within the city, first mentioned in 1294, 800 Jews lived in Vienna during the Middle Ages. Merchants, bankers and scholars, Judenplatz was the centre of their activities. In addition to a hospital, the square was the site of a synagogue and school. Just around the corner from Judenplatz is the street called Kurrentgasse, where the tax-collectors resided. The Jewish city is bounded in the north by a church: Maria am Gestade. In the Middle Ages, this church stood directly on the banks of the Danube. Danube boatmen, approaching on their barges, were able to recognise the majestic church towers from a long way off. Ottakringer Bach, a stream from the northwest, flows directly beside the church, and the weavers and dyers would use the water in their work; later the brook was diverted. The former brookbed was never completely filled, and today its outlines can be recognised in the street known as Tiefer Graben (Deep Trench). Nowadays one can also take in the medieval atmosphere in the vicinity of the little street named Schönlaterngasse. The narrow, winding lanes veritably breathe the spirit of the past.

links: Gotische Kirche Maria am Gestade (14./15. Jh.),
und mittelalterliche Häuser mit Renaissancefassaden
rechts: Judenplatz mit gotischem Bürgerhaus
left: Gothic church Maria am Gestade (14th/15th century),
medieval buildings with Renaissance facades on the right
right: Judenplatz with Gothic burgher house

Der Stephansdom
St. Stephan's Cathedral

Er ist Wiens Kathedrale – die Wiener nennen ihn liebevoll „Steffl". Die Anfänge des geschichtsträchtigen Gebäudes gehen auf das Jahr 1137 zurück, als hier ein romanischer Bau entstand. Dem folgte ein zweiter, von dem heute noch die Westfassade erhalten ist. 1359 legt Rudolf VI. dann den Grundstein zur gotischen Erweiterung der Kirche und es wird ein Neubau mit Errichtung einer lichten, dreischiffigen Chorhalle begonnen. Die Kirche sollte ursprünglich zwei gleich hohe Türme bekommen, und der Erste der beiden, der Südturm, wurde 1433 vollendet. Das gotische Langhaus wurde 1474 fertiggestellt und wurde wie eine Zwiebelschale über das romanische Langhaus gebaut, das dann abgerissen werden konnte. Bereits 1450 wurde der Grundstein für den Nordturm gelegt. Dieser Turm war allerdings zu groß und prunkvoll konzipiert, außerdem neigte sich die Zeit der gotischen Kathedralen dem Ende zu. Und so kam es, dass die Bauarbeiten schließlich 1511 eingestellt wurden und der Turmstumpf 1578 mit einer Renaissance-Haube abgeschlossen wurde. Gegen Ende des 15. Jahrhunderts wurde St. Stephan zur Kathedrale, also zu einem Bischofssitz und seit 1723 ist der Dom der Sitz des Erzbischofs von Wien. Der unvollendete Nordturm beherbergt mit der „Pummerin" die zweitgrößte freischwingende Glocke Europas.

12
13

The cathedral of Vienna is amiably termed *Steffl* (Stevie) by regular worshippers. The beginnings of this historical building go back to the year 1137, when a Roman building still stood on the site. A second edifice followed, and the western facade has survived to the present. The cornerstone for expanding the church in the Gothic style was laid by Rudolf VI in 1359, and construction of a bright new choir hall with three naves commenced. The church was originally designed with two towers of equal height, and the first of these, the south tower, was completed in 1433. The Gothic nave, completed in 1474, was erected similar to a bell over the Roman nave, which was subsequently demolished. The cornerstone for the north tower was laid as early as 1450. Yet, this tower was planned to be too large and opulent, while the age of Gothic cathedrals had begun to draw to a close. Thus, building activities were brought to a standstill in 1511, and the tower stump was capped with a Renaissance hood in 1578. In the latter 15th century, St. Stephan was elevated to the status of cathedral, i.e. it became a bishop's see, and it has been the see of the Archbishop of Vienna since 1723. The incomplete north tower is the home of the Pummerin bell, the second largest freely swinging bell in Europe.

Stephansdom mit Westfassade
St. Stephan's Cathedral with western facade

Barock und Palais
Baroque and palaces

Nach dem Jahr 1683 sonnen sich die Wiener im Licht des zweiten Sieges über die Türken. Und dieses Ereignis beflügelt. Aus dem mittelalterlichen, ummauerten Herzogssitz entwickelt sich „Vienna Gloriosa", die glanzvolle imperiale Metropole, das Zentrum hochbarocker Kultur. Begonnen hatte der Aufbruch ins Barockzeitalter allerdings schon knapp vor der Türkenbelagerung, als Kaiser Leopold I. den Bau des Leopoldinischen Traktes der Hofburg in Auftrag gab. Dieser barocke Palastbau setzt ein Zeichen für den Wiener Adel: Wer adelig ist, will sich mit einem barocken Palast ein Denkmal setzen. Das Wiener Palais – oder besser gesagt viele davon – entstehen auf engstem Raum, denn es ist verboten, die damalige Stadtmauer und das Glacis zu verbauen. Der einfache Ausweg: Man kauft mehrere Bürgerhäuser und reißt sie ab, um Platz zu schaffen.

Following the year 1683, Vienna is revelling in the wake of its second victory over the Turks. And this event provides drive. From the medieval seat of the duchy, surrounded by walls, *Vienna gloriosa* emerges, the dazzling imperial capital, the centre of high Baroque culture. Yet, Vienna had already begun to enter the Baroque age just before the Turkish siege, when Emperor Leopold I commissioned erection of the Leopoldine Wing of the Hofburg. This Baroque palace structure sent out a signal to Vienna's nobility: a true noble has a Baroque palace built as a monument to them. These palaces, a substantial number in fact, are built within narrow confines, as the erection of buildings adjoining the city walls or the glacis (adjacent embankment) is prohibited. The simplest solution is to buy up several burgher residences and tear them down to make room for palaces. A bustle of building activity develops after 1683, and Vienna in the Baroque period becomes a city of palaces. Among the factors augmenting the number are the aristocratic families from everywhere in Europe that move here, to a city considered to be of such great political importance, with hopes of climbing the social ladder. By 1730, Vienna already numbers 238 palaces and residences of nobles and aristocrats, amounting to a full quarter of all buildings.

Nach 1683 entwickelt sich eine rege Bautätigkeit und das barocke Wien entwickelt sich zu einer Stadt der Palais. Zu so vielen Neubauten kommt es auch deswegen, weil sich Adelsfamilien aus ganz Europa in einer politisch so wichtigen Stadt den gesellschaftlichen Aufstieg versprechen. Um 1730 gibt es in Wien bereits 238 Adelspaläste und Herrschaftshäuser, das ist ein Viertel des Baubestandes.

Palais Harrach / Palais Harrach
Palais Kinsky / Palais Kinsky

Wien im Wandel
Vienna in changing times

Mittelalter
Middle Ages

Barock
Baroque

Gründerzeit
Mittel Gründ period

Der Weg in ein neues Zeitalter hat begonnen, die Einwohnerzahl Wiens steigt ständig, alleine zwischen 1750 und 1790 von 175.000 auf 235.000. Das verändert die Stadt innerhalb von kurzer Zeit extrem, auch baulich. Sie wird neu strukturiert. Viele mittelalterliche Gassen verschwinden oder werden umgebaut, sternförmige Achsen nach außen wie die Wollzeile entstehen, die strengen Formen der Renaissance werden aufgelockert, die hohen, breiten Häuser des Barock mit reich verzierten Fassaden halten Einzug. Aber nicht nur die neuentstandenen Palais kennzeichnen das barocke Stadtbild, auch viele mittelalterliche Gebäude erhalten eine neue, barocke Fassade. Palais repräsentieren nicht nur den Adel, sondern sie schmücken auch die Viertel, in denen sie liegen. „Am Hof" zum Beispiel strotzt nur so vor Prachtbauten. Im Speziellen anziehend ist die Freyung. Dort gibt es Platz, weil ein Brand im Zuge der zweiten Türkenbelagerung die meisten Gebäude vernichtet hat. Darum finden sich hier neben der Daun-Kinsky-Wohnstätte auch die Palais Harrach und Ferstel. Als Bilderbuchpalais gilt das Palais Daun-Kinsky. Seine Fassade ist bis weit ins 19. Jahrhundert hinein stilbildend.

A new era had been ushered in Vienna's population continues to grow, from 175,000 to 235,000 between 1750 and 1790 alone. This growth has an enormous impact on the city within a short period, in architectural terms as well. The city is restructured. Many medieval streets disappear or are rerouted; star-shaped axes branching out from the centre, such as the Wollzeile, are defined; and the strict forms of the Renaissance dissolve, giving way to tall, broad Baroque edifices with sumptuously decorated facades. Yet, not only do the newly erected palaces dominate the appearance of the Baroque city. A number of medieval buildings are also fitted with a new, Baroque facade. Palaces adorn their erectors. That is obvious. Yet they adorn not only the nobility but also the quarter where they are situated. The Am Hof square, to cite an example, is literally bursting with lavish edifices. And the Freyung square is particularly attractive. Space has been made there by a fire, destroying most of the buildings, during the second Turkish siege. For this reason, Palais Harrach and Palais Ferstel, in addition to the Daun-Kinsky residence, are located here. Palais Daun-Kinsky is considered an ideal palace construction. The palace facade served as a model for architectural styles well on into the 19th century.

Die Freyung/The Freyung square

Barocke Kirchen
Baroque churches

Peterskirche / Peterskirche
Karlskirche / Karlskirche

Die Barockisierung Wiens wurde ganz stark durch weltliche Gebäude geprägt. Und weil der Barock in Wien länger als anderswo dauert, erlebt auch die sakrale Architektur einen Höhepunkt. Wiens Barockkirchen zählen nicht nur zu den schönsten, man findet auch an kaum einem Ort eine größere Dichte. Über allen anderen steht die Karlskirche. Im Jahr 1713, nach der letzten großen Pestepidemie, gelobte Kaiser Karl VI., eine Kirche für den Pestheiligen Karl Borromäus zu bauen. In dem 1737 fertiggestellten Sakralbau vereinigt Johann Bernhard Fischer von Erlach auf unnachahmliche Weise die klassische Architektur Roms, Griechenlands und Konstantinopels. So erinnern die Seitentürme an orientalische Pagoden, während die hohen Säulen, die das griechische Portal umrahmen, islamischen Minaretten wie auch römischen Triumphsäulen gleichen. Ein anderes Beispiel ist die Peterskirche, deren Existenz auf Karl den Großen zurückgehen soll und deren barocker Neubau bestätigt, dass viele Köche nicht zwangsweise den Brei verderben. Die Pläne dafür entwirft Gabriele Montanis, Lukas von Hildebrandt verändert sie zum Teil und die letztlich durchgeführte Fassadenlösung soll Kilian Ignaz Dientzenhofer in einem Brief angeregt haben. Die Kirche wird 1722 fertiggestellt und ist der erste Kuppelbau des barocken Wiens.

Vienna's metamorphosis into a Baroque city was strongly driven by secular buildings. And, since the Baroque period lasts longer than elsewhere, religious architecture is developed to a climax. Not only are Vienna's Baroque churches among the most beautiful, hardly anywhere else is there a greater concentration. The Karlskirche stands at the pinnacle of these churches. In the year 1713, following the last great plague, Emperor Karl VI vowed to erect a church in honour of the plague saint Carlo Borromeo. In this religious edifice, completed in 1737, Johann Bernhard Fischer von Erlach united the classical architecture of Rome, Greece and Constantinople in an incomparable fashion. Thus, the towers at the side are reminiscent of oriental pagodas, while the tall columns framing the Greek portal call to mind at once both Muslim minarets and Roman victory columns. The Peterskirche is yet another example. The existence of the church is attributed to Charlemagne, and the Baroque reconstruction demonstrates that many cooks don't necessarily spoil the broth. While Gabriele Montanis drew up the plans, Lukas von Hildebrandt partly modified them, and Kilian Ignaz Dientzenhofer is said to have in a letter provided the suggestion for the facade solution that was lastly implemented. Completed in 1722, the church became the first domed structure in Baroque Vienna.

Schloss Belvedere
Belvedere Palace

If Prince Eugen von Savoyen, the most important field marshal of the early 18th century, desires a palace adjacent to the Vienna inner city, situated among picturesque gardens, then he shall have it. He has it built in the years 1714 to 1723. The name: Belvedere. The prince entrusts Johann Lukas von Hildebrandt with the erection of the upper palace and Giovanni Stanetti with the lower palace. Jointly they create a lavish ensemble of parks and palace buildings, including an orangerie and a menagerie. The Lower Belvedere is a long, single-storey structure featuring a portal similar to a victory arch and windows extending almost to the floor. The Upper Belvedere, consisting of three storeys and four eight-sided corner pavilions, is a classic example of the Baroque architecture of the time, one of the reasons it was named a world heritage site. While the prince resided in the Lower Belvedere, the structure above was used for official occasions. After the death of Prince Eugen in 1781, the Habsburgs took over the palace, and they used it as an imperial painting gallery as well as a family residence. In 1955 the Austrian State Treaty was signed at the Upper Belvedere. Today the Upper Belvedere is the home of the Austrian Gallery Belvedere, whereas temporary exhibitions are on display at the lower palace.

Wenn sich der wichtigste Feldherr des frühen 18. Jahrhunderts, Prinz Eugen von Savoyen, ein Schloss am Rand der Wiener Innenstadt mitten in einer herrlichen Gartenanlage wünscht, dann soll er es bekommen. 1714–1723 lässt er es bauen. Sein Name: Belvedere. Den Bau des oberen Schlosses legt er in Johann Lukas von Hildebrandts Hände, den des unteren in die von Giovanni Stanetti. Zusammen schaffen sie eine prunkvolle Park- und Schlossanlage mit Orangerie und Menagerie. Das untere Belvedere zeigt sich als eingeschossiger Langbau mit triumphbogenähnlichem Portal und fast bis zum Boden reichenden Fenstern. Das dreigeschossige obere Belvedere mit vier achteckigen Eckpavillions ist ein Musterbeispiel der damaligen Barockbaukunst, weswegen es auch als Weltkulturerbe anerkannt wurde. Der Prinz lebt allerdings im unteren Belvedere, während das obere Bauwerk Repräsentationszwecken dient. Nach dem Tod von Prinz Eugen 1781 fällt das Schloss an die Habsburger, die es als kaiserliche Gemäldegalerie, aber auch als Familiensitz verwenden. 1955 wird im oberen Belvedere der Staatsvertrag unterzeichnet. Heute beherbergt das obere Belvedere die „Österreichische Galerie Belvedere", während im unteren Belvedere wechselnde Ausstellungen gezeigt werden.

Oberes Schloss Belvedere
The Upper Belvedere Palace

Die Ringstraße
Ringstraße (Ring Street)

„Es ist mein Wille", mit diesen Worten leitet Kaiser Franz Joseph I. im Dezember 1857 ein kaiserliches Handschreiben ein, das Wien einmal mehr verändern wird. Er verfügt die längst überfällige Schleifung der Basteien und eine planmäßige, großzügige Erweiterung der Stadt. Mit der Abtragung der Mauern und der Verbauung des Glacis soll die Barriere zwischen der Inneren Stadt und den Vorstädten wegfallen. Verbinden sollen beide ein breiter Kai am Donaukanal und ein halbkreisförmiger Boulevard um die Innere Stadt. Finanziell möglich macht das Vorhaben der Stadterweiterungs-

fonds, der sich aus dem Verkauf der durch das Schleifen neu entstandenen Bauparzellen speist. Das erste repräsentative öffentliche Gebäude, die Hofoper, legt den Grundstein zum Mythos „Ringstraßenära". Architektonisch ist diese, abgesehen von wenigen secessionistischen Gebäuden, mit dem klassischen und späten Historismus, ökonomisch mit der Gründerzeit identisch. Eröffnet wird die rund 4 km lange, 57 m breite von Alleen gesäumte Prachtstraße am 1. Mai 1865, vollendet aber erst kurz vor dem Ersten Weltkrieg.

"It is my will": with these words Emperor Franz Joseph I begins an imperial autograph in December 1857 which will yet once more change the face of Vienna. He decrees the long-overdue razing of the city ramparts *(Basteien)* and a generous expansion of the city according to plan. Demolishing the walls and the glacis is intended to remove the barrier between the inner city and the suburbs. The two areas are to be connected by a broad quay along the Danube Canal and an arc-shaped boulevard surrounding the inner city. A financial prerequisite for the project is the *Stadterweiterungsfonds*, the city expansion fund which is funded by the proceeds from the sale of the new building lots created by razing the walls. The first stately public building, the Hofoper (Court Opera), laid the foundation for the legendary "Ring Street Era". With the exception of a few secessionist buildings, the architectural style of the era is identical with classical and late historicism, while the economic period is the same as that of the Wilhelminian period. The stately boulevard, with a length of some four kilometres and a width of 57 metres, bounded by avenues, is inaugurated on 1 May 1865, whereas final completion must wait until just before the First World War.

Ringstraße: Hofburg (r.u.), Kunst- und Naturhistorisches Museum (l.), Parlament (o.) und Rathaus (r.o.)
Ringstraße: Hofburg (below right), Art History Museum and Natural History Museum (left), Parliament (top) and City Hall (top right)

Historismus
Historicism

Neogotik, Neorenaissance, Neobarock. Dazu kommen ab 1870 noch die Neoromanik und im zweiten Drittel des 19. Jahrhunderts das Neorokoko als beliebter Einrichtungsstil in Schlössern und Bürgerhäusern. Der Historismus – das Aufgreifen ästhetischer Formen der Vergangenheit – repetiert die ganze abendländische Baugeschichte der frühen Neuzeit. Von einfachem Nachahmen kann man aber nicht sprechen, vielmehr von subjektiven Interpretationen, denn die neue Zeit fordert neue Gebäude. Zur Linderung der aus der Urbanisierung entstandenen Wohnungsnot braucht es mehrstöckige Zinshäuser. Das aufstrebende und zusehends wohlhabende Bürgertum verlangt nach prachtvolleren Villen und Stadtwohnungen in repräsentativen Gebäuden, deren typisches Zeichen später ihre Stockwerk für Stockwerk unterschiedlich gestalteten Fensterreihen sein werden. Die beginnende Industrielle Revolution wiederum erfordert den Bau von Bahnhöfen, Fabriken und Wassertürmen. In Wien werden ganze Stadtviertel dem Muster des Historismus folgend gebaut. Und auch vor den entlang der Ringstraße angesiedelten öffentlichen Gebäuden macht er nicht halt. Man denke nur an die Staatsoper im Stil der Neorenaissance, das Parlamentsgebäude in einem neo-attischen Stil, oder das Rathaus im Stil der Flämischen Gotik.

Neo-Gothic, neo-Renaissance, neo-Baroque. These are joined by neo-Romanesque, after 1870, and by neo-Rococo, a favoured style for furnishing palaces and manors, in the second third of the 19th century. Historicism, i.e. the revival of aesthetic forms from a past era, is a practice found throughout the early modern period of Western architectural history. This is not simply a case of emulation but instead involves subjective interpretation. After all, a new era demands new buildings. Apartment houses with several storeys are needed to meet the housing shortage caused by urbanisation. The burghers, rising in society and attaining increasing wealth, have an appetite for even more lavish villas and town flats in stately buildings; the typical feature of these buildings will later come to be the rows of windows styled differently in each storey. Moreover, the Industrial Revolution, just underway, requires construction of train stations, factories and water towers. In Vienna, entire city districts are erected in accordance with the historicist pattern. Nor are the public edifices lining the Ringstraße excluded from this trend. The examples that came to mind in this regard: the State Opera designed in the Renaissance revival style; the Parliament Building, erected in neo-Attic style; and the City Hall as styled in Flemish Gothic.

Parlament, Staatsoper, Rathaus, Naturhistorisches Museum
Parliament, State Opera, City Hall, Natural History Museum

Prunk und Pracht
Splendour and luxury

Dem Prachtboulevard Ringstraße wird eine „Lastenstraße" entgegengesetzt. Umgangssprachlich nach der dort lange verkehrenden Straßenbahn noch heute als „2er Linie" bezeichnet, verläuft sie in einem annähernden Halbkreis ausgehend vom Karlsplatz stadtauswärts parallel zum Ring. Der Raum zwischen Ring und Lastenstraße bietet nicht nur Platz für die Monumentalbauten, sondern auch für zahlreiche prächtige Wohnhäuser. Doch noch einmal zur Pracht: Neben der Ringstraße punktet damit zunehmend auch der „Graben". Im Zug der Babenbergischen Stadterweiterung im 12. Jahrhundert zugeschüttet und planiert, hatte er noch bis ins 18. Jahrhundert hinein als Markt gedient. Anfang des 19. Jahrhunderts siedeln sich hier aber immer mehr Luxusgeschäfte an. Zwischen 1860 und 1866 fallen dann zahlreiche Häuser zwischen Grabengasse und Schlossergassl. Der Graben geht nun direkt in den Stock-im-Eisen-Platz bzw. den Stephansplatz über. Historismusgeprägte Gebäude finden sich auch hier. Der Grabenhof etwa, ein Werk Otto Thienemanns und Otto Wagners. Letztgenannter nimmt mit dem ebenfalls dort gelegenen „Ankerhaus" sogar seine Zukunft vorweg. Die Art des Untergeschosses mit seinen Glasflächen weist auf spätere Baustrukturen hin, wie er sie als Secessionist in Stahlbetonbauten verwenden wird.

Graben: Barock trifft Gründerzeit. Peterskirche, barocke Pestsäule und typische Wohnhäuser der Gründerzeit
Graben: Baroque and Wilhelminian periods. Peterskirche, baroque Pestsäule and typical residential buildings dating back to the Wilhelminian period

The Ringstraße, a stately boulevard, receives a *Lastenstraße* (lit. "load road") as a counterpart. Commonly referred to still today as the "2er Linie", for the tramway line that long serviced the route, the *Lastenstraße* runs away from the city and parallel to the Ring in a rough semi-circle beginning from Karlsplatz. The space between the Ring and the *Lastenstraße* provides space both for monumental edifices, as well as numerous luxurious residential buildings. But let us return to the subject of splendour: next to the Ringstraße, this is also becoming a characteristic of the street called Graben. Filled in during the Babenberg expansion of the city in the 12th century, the former trench served as a marketplace as late as the 18th century. A growing number of luxury shops are set up in the early 19th century. Later, between 1860 and 1866, a large number of buildings between Grabengasse and Schlossergassl are razed. Now the Graben merges directly with Stock im Eisen Platz and Stephansplatz. Buildings marked by historicism are also found here. The Grabenhof, for one, is the work of Otto Thienemann and Otto Wagner. In designing the Ankerhaus, the latter anticipates his own future, in fact. The appearance of the lower storey, with its glass surfaces, points the way to later structures in reinforced concrete which Wagner would erect as a member of the Secession.

Jugendstil

Jugendstil

Mittelalter
Middle Ages
Barock
Baroque
Gründerzeit
Wilhelminian period

Wildly combining styles and functions goes too far for the avant-garde. They create Jugendstil, a style which presents new forms for all areas of art as an alternative to historicism. The design of an object is developed from its material and function. Clear forms and lines, floral ornaments covering entire surfaces – that is what appeals to the artists who join together under the leadership of Hermann Bahr and Gustav Klimt to form the Vienna Secession. When they commission the architect Joseph Maria Olbrich, not even 30 years old, to erect an exhibition building, as expected, Olbrich declares the end of historicist architecture. Cubes, smoothly folded inside one another and stuccoed white, ornamented by vegetation and geometric figures, and crowned by a dome in the form of a forged laurel tree plated with genuine gold: that is the Secession. No less worthy of note is Otto Wagner's k.k. Postsparcassen-Amt (Royal and Imperial Post Office Savings Bank Bureau), built in the years 1904 to 1906 using the new material of reinforced concrete and with a facade dressed in marble panels and aluminium plates. Numerous additional Jugendstil buildings are then erected in Vienna. Yet some take exception to Jugendstil. Adolf Loos for one, a precursor of the modern style and a proponent of a brand of purism that, aesthetically radical, refuses ornamentation.

Das wilde Kombinieren von Stilen und Funktionen wird der Avantgarde zu viel. Sie setzt dem Historismus mit dem Jugendstil neue Formen für alle Bereiche der Kunst und des Lebens entgegen. Aus Material und Funktion eines Gegenstandes wird das Design entwickelt. Klare Formen und Linien, florale flächige Ornamente – das mögen die Künstler, die sich unter der Führung von Hermann Bahr und Gustav Klimt zur „Wiener Secession" zusammenschließen. Als sie den kaum 30jährigen Architekten Joseph Maria Olbrich mit einem Ausstellungsgebäude beauftragen, erteilt dieser der Architektur des Historismus die erwünschte Absage. Glatte ineinander verschachtelte Kuben, weiß verputzt, mit vegetativen und geometrischen Ornamenten und eine geschmiedete, echt vergoldete Kuppel eines Lorbeerbaums als Krönung: Das ist die Secession. Ihr in nichts nachstehend ist Otto Wagners zwischen 1904 und 1906 in einer neuen Stahlbetonweise gebautes k.k. Postsparcassen-Amt, dessen Fassade mit quadratischen Marmortäfelchen und Aluminiumapplikationen belegt ist. Zahlreiche weitere Jugendstilgebäude entstehen nun in Wien. Doch auch am Jugendstil reibt sich mancher. Adolf Loos etwa, Vorreiter der Moderne und Verfechter des radikal ästhetischen ornamentlosen Purismus.

Secession, Postsparkasse
Secession, Postsparkasse

Die Hofburg im Mittelalter
The Hofburg in the Middle Ages

Wenn ein Gebäude über 600 Jahre lang Landesfürsten als Residenz dient, dann darf es sich mit Fug und Recht „geschichtsträchtig" nennen. Bei der Wiener Hofburg ist das so. In der Hofburg kann man die drei wichtigsten Kulturepochen – Mittelalter, Barock und Gründerzeit – in einem Gebäudekomplex bewundern. Sie beherbergte einst die Habsburger und ist heute der Amtssitz des österreichischen Bundespräsidenten. Erstgenannte wohnten dort als Landesherren und Kaiser. Die mittelalterliche befestigte Burganlage des 13. Jahrhunderts wurde ständig um neue Trakte oder Flügel erweitert. So lange, bis aus ihr eine eigene „Stadt in der Stadt" wurde. Gesamt erstreckt sich der asymmetrische Komplex über 240.000 m², 18 Trakte mit 2.600 Räumen – in denen jetzt noch rund 5.000 Menschen wohnen und arbeiten – und 19 Höfe. Der älteste Teil ist die alte Burg, die seit dem 18. Jahrhundert nach der dort als Burgwache tätigen Schweizergarde „Schweizertrakt" genannt wird. Bis jetzt ist die mittelalterliche Burganlage im Kern erhalten, nur die vier Ecktürme und Teile des Burggrabens wurden im Lauf der Zeit erneuert und die Fassade glänzt seit Mitte des 16. Jahrhunderts im Renaissancestil. Passend dazu baute Pietro Ferabosco 1552 mit dem Schweizertor übrigens eines der wenigen Wiener Renaissancedenkmäler.

Hofburg von oben / Hofburg from above
Schweizertor / Swiss Gate

An edifice that serves as the residence of a country's rulers for more than 600 years has every right to be termed historic. Such is the case with the Vienna Hofburg. Austria's three most important cultural epochs, that is the Middle Ages, Baroque and the Wilhelminian period, can be admired in one building complex. Once home to the Habsburgers, today it houses the offices of the Federal President of Austria. The former resided there as territorial rulers and emperors. The medieval castle complex, built in the 13th century, was continuously expanded with the addition of new sections and wings. This continued until it became of itself a "city within the city". The asymmetrical complex is spread over an area of 240,000 m² and encompasses 18 wings and 2,600 rooms, in which today around 5,000 people still work and live, and 19 courtyards. The oldest section is the old fortress, named Schweizertrakt after the Swiss Guard that stood duty there, guarding the castle. The core of the medieval castle complex has been preserved to the present, with the exception of the four corner towers and castle moat section, which were renovated in the course of time, and the facade, which has been shining in Renaissance lustre since the mid-16th century. In harmony with the face, Pietro Ferabosco erected the Schweizertor or Swiss Gate in 1552, now one of Vienna's few Renaissance monuments.

Die barocke Hofburg
The Baroque Hofburg

Die Barock-Repräsentanten der Hofburg sind der Leopoldinische Trakt aus dem 17., der Reichskanzleitrakt aus dem 18. und der im 19. Jahrhundert im Neubarock fertiggestellte Michaelertrakt. Der von Kaiser Leopold I. in den 1660er-Jahren beauftragte frühbarocke Leopoldinische Trakt verbindet den Schweizertrakt mit der Amalienburg. Im 18. Jahrhundert bewohnt ihn Maria Theresia, seit 1946 residiert hier der Bundespräsident. Ebenfalls bekennender Barock-Anhänger ist Kaiser Karl VI. An seiner Seite: Joseph Bernhard Fischer von Erlach und sein Sohn Johann Emanuel, der nach Vaters Plänen baut – etwa die Nationalbibliothek samt Prunksaal. Nach dessen Tod wird von Lukas von Hildebrandt der Reichskanzleitrakt errichtet, in dem später Kaiser Franz Joseph leben wird. Johann Emanuel Fischer von Erlach plant 1726 auch den Michaelertrakt, die Verbindung zwischen Winterreitschule und Reichskanzleitrakt. Doch erst 1889, nachdem das alte Hofburgtheater abgetragen wurde und das Theater an den Ring übersiedelt, wird mit dem Bau des Michaelertraktes begonnen und der barocke Bau wird beinahe 200 Jahre nach seiner Planung 1893 in leicht veränderter Form fertiggestellt.

The sections of the Hofburg representing the Baroque style are the 17th-century Leopoldine Wing, the Reichskanzleitrakt (Imperial Chancellery Wing), originating in the 18th century, and the neo-Baroque Michaelertrakt or St. Michael Wing, which was completed in the 19th century. In the 1660s, Emperor Leopold I has the Schweizertrakt joined with the Amalienburg residence. The resulting Leopoldine Wing in the early Baroque style is apparently attractive: Maria Theresia resides here in the 18th century, and it has housed the Austrian Federal President since 1946. Emperor Karl VI is also an espoused devotee of Baroque. At his side: court architect Joseph Bernhard Fischer von Erlach and his son Johann Emanuel, who executes his father's plans, resulting in the National Library with its Prunksaal or Great Hall, to name one example. After his death, Lukas von Hildebrandt erects the Imperial Chancellery Wing, where Emperor Franz Joseph will later take up residence. Johann Emanuel Fischer von Erlach also draws up plans for the St. Michael Wing in 1726, the section connecting the Winter Riding School and the Imperial Chancellery Wing. Yet the old Hofburg Theatre stands in the way of the new wing. It was not until 1889, after the theatre building is demolished and the theatre relocated in the new building on the Ring, that construction of the St. Michael Wing begins. The Baroque structure is subsequently completed in 1893, almost 200 years after the plans were drawn up, in somewhat modified form.

Innerer Burghof mit Amalienburg und Reichskanzleitrakt Inner bailey incl. Amalienburg and Imperial Chancellery Wing

Die Hofburg der Gründerzeit
The Hofburg – Wilhelminian period

Wien wächst und so kommt es im Zuge der Stadterweiterung in den 1860er Jahren zur letzten großen Erweiterung der Hofburg. Geplant ist eine zweiflügelige Anlage über die Ringstraße hinweg, das „Kaiserforum". Zwillingsmuseen (Kunsthistorisches und Naturhistorisches Museum) sollen als Flanken dienen, die Hofstallungen von Fischer von Erlach den Abschluss bilden. Gottfried Semper leitet das Projekt, später übernimmt Karl Freiherr von Hasenauer. Doch es kommt anders. Zwar bringt man den Museen-Bau 1891 zum Abschluss, die Bauarbeiten für den Rest des Forums ziehen sich aber quälend langsam dahin. Und zwar so lange, bis das Kaiserforum nach der Fertigstellung des Südostflügels der Hofburg, der Neuen Burg, ad acta gelegt wird. Der Heldenplatz in seiner heutigen Form entsteht. Monumentale Reiterstatuen der beiden bedeutenden österreichischen Feldherren Prinz Eugen und Erzherzog Karl schmücken den Platz, abgeschlossen wird er zum Ring hin vom Heldentor. Der Trakt der Neuen Burg wird allerdings niemals bewohnt, das Ende der Monarchie und der Erste Weltkrieg verhindern das. Heute befinden sich unter anderem das Völkerkundemuseum und der Lesesaal der Nationalbibliothek in der Neuen Burg.

As Vienna grows, the last major expansion of the Hofburg takes place as part of civic expansion activities in the 1860s. A complex encompassing two wings and spanning the Ringstraße is planned: the Kaiserforum. Twin museums, the Art History and the Natural History museums, are to flank the complex and the old court stables by Fischer von Erlach will complete the group. Gottfried Semper leads the project, which later Karl Freiherr von Hasenauer takes over. Yet the outcome is another. While construction of the museums is completed in 1891, work on the remainder of the forum drags on at an excruciating pace. This state of affairs continues until, following completion of the south-eastern wing of the Hofburg, the New Burg, the Imperial Forum is finally abandoned. The result is the Heldenplatz in its present form. The square is adorned by monumental statues of horsemen, representing the two renowned Austrian field marshals Prince Eugen and Archduke Karl, while the Heldentor or Heroes' Gate forms a boundary to the Ring. No one comes to reside in the wing formed by the New Burg; the end of the monarchy and the First World War prevent this. Today, the New Burg houses the Museum of Ethnology and the reading hall of the National Library along with other facilities.

Neue Hofburg / New Hofburg

Schönbrunn – das Schloss
Schönbrunn – the palace

Die Legende sagt: Es war ein Brunnen mit besonders klarem Wasser, der Schönbrunn seinen Namen gegeben hat. Wahr ist: Maximilian II. kauft das Anwesen mit der Bezeichnung „Katterburg" . Leopold I. engagiert 1687 Johann Bernhard Fischer von Erlach, an deren Stelle ein Schloss zu bauen. 1700 vollendet dieser den Mitteltrakt, dann bremst ihn der Spanische Erbfolgekrieg, der Bau bleibt bis Maria Theresias Regentschaft unvollendet. Diese holt sich Architekt Nikolaus Pacassi an ihre Seite und ließ ihn 1743–1749 das Schloss entscheidend erweitern und umbauen. Maria Theresia nutzt Schönbrunn als ihre kaiserliche Sommerresidenz und lässt 1747 ein eigenes Schlosstheater im nördlichen Hoftrakt erbauen. Ihr Tod leert das Schloss und erst Anfang des 19. Jahrhunderts wird es durch Kaiser Franz II./I. wieder bewohnt. Dieser lässt Schönbrunn renovieren, nachdem Napoleon es 1805 und 1809 besetzt hat. Nach dem Wiener Kongress 1814/15 wird die Rokokoverkleidung entfernt. Auch das berühmte „Schönbrunner Gelb" entsteht wahrscheinlich in dieser Zeit, das Schloss erhält ein neues Gesicht und erlebt ab 1848 noch einmal eine glänzende Zeit als Habsburger Herrschaftsresidenz. Kaiser Franz Joseph I., der 1830 in Schönbrunn geboren wird, verbringt einen Großteil seiner Zeit in diesem wunderbaren Prunkbau.

It was a spring with unusually clear water, so the legend goes, that gave Schönbrunn (lit. fair spring) its name. The truth is, Maximilian II purchases the estate as the Katterburg mansion. In 1687 Leopold I hires Bernhard Fischer von Erlach to erect a palace to replace it. The architect completes the centre wing in 1700, after which progress is halted by the War of the Spanish Succession, and the palace is not completed until the time of Maria Theresia. The empress calls the architect Nikolaus Pacassi to her court and gives him the task of expanding and restructuring the palace to a considerable extent from 1743 to 1749. Maria Theresia uses the palace as her imperial summer residence. She has a separate palace theatre built in the north wing in 1747. With her death the palace is emptied of life, and not until the beginning of the 19th century does Emperor Franz II/I again take up residence. After the occupation of Schönbrunn by Napoleon in 1805 and 1809, Franz has the palace renovated. The Rococo decoration is removed following the Congress of Vienna in the years 1814 to 1815. It is likely that the famous Schönbrunn yellow of the outside walls also goes back to this period. Schönbrunn receives a facelift and later, after 1848, experiences a new golden age as the residence of the Habsburg rulers. Emperor Franz Joseph I, born at Schönbrunn in 1830, spends much of his time at this beautiful palace.

Schloss Schönbrunn / Schönbrunn Palace

Schönbrunn – der Park
Schönbrunn – the park

Extending over an area of about 1.2 km by 1 km, the palace park of Schönbrunn is among the most beautiful Baroque gardens in existence. For this reason the park is included, together with Schönbrunn Palace, in the list of world heritage sites. A splendid garden came into existence already under Leopold I, but it was devastated in 1683 by the Ottoman Turks. Franz I Stephan von Lothringen brought the gardens to bloom once again. The husband of Maria Theresia expanded the estate and structured it, introduced a new system of alleys in the shape of a star. The palace and the park form a unity. According to the principles of Baroque garden architecture and art, the garden serves as an extension of the interior rooms. At the centre of the gardens is the Great Parterre, with flower beds laid out in artistic patterns. The end of the Parterre is bounded by the impressive Neptune Fountain, opposite the palace, with its larger-than-life statues. Behind the fountain, a hill slopes upward to where the Gloriette thrones. Among the other attractions of the grounds are the artificial Roman ruins, erected in 1778, and the Obelisk Fountain, completed in 1777. Somewhat off to the side one finds a structure that since 1771 has housed the Schöner Brunnen or Fair Spring, which gives the palace its name. In the years 1880 to 1882, the Great Palm House is erected in the park.

Der Schlosspark von Schönbrunn gehört mit seiner Ausdehnung von etwa 1,2 km in der Länge und 1 km in der Breite zu den schönsten Barockgärten, die es gibt. Deswegen wurde er auch gemeinsam mit dem Schloss in die Liste des Welterbes aufgenommen. Schon unter Leopold I. entsteht hier ein prächtiger Garten, der jedoch 1683 von den Osmanen verwüstet wird. Wieder erblühen lässt ihn Franz I. Stephan von Lothringen. Maria Theresias Ehemann erweitert die Anlage und gliedert sie durch ein neues sternförmiges Alleensystem. Schloss und Park bilden eine Einheit. Den Prinzipien der barocken Gartenbaukunst zufolge dient der Garten als Fortsetzung der Innenräume. Das Zentrum des Parks bildet das „Große Parterre" mit seinen kunstvoll angelegten Blumenbeeten. Am Ende des Parterres, gegenüber vom Schloss findet diese Fläche durch den beeindruckenden Neptunbrunnen mit seinen überlebensgroßen Figuren seinen Abschluss. Hinter dem Brunnen beginnt der Hügel, auf dem die Gloriette thront. Weitere Höhepunkte bilden eine künstliche römische Ruine, die 1778 errichtet wurde, und der 1777 vollendete „Obeliskbrunnen". Ein wenig abseits steht seit 1771 ein Gebäude, das den namensgebenden „Schönen Brunnen" beherbergt. 1880–1882 entsteht im Park das große Palmenhaus.

Schönbrunn – der Park: Gloriette, Neptunbrunnen, Rundbassin, Palmenhaus / Schönbrunn – the park: Gloriette, Neptun Fountain, Round Pool, Palm House

Schönbrunn – der Tiergarten
Schönbrunn – the zoo

Weil Franz I. Stephan nicht nur Flora-, sondern auch Fauna-interessiert ist, lässt er Architekt Nicolas Jadot 1751 eine Tiergartenanlage in Form von 13 radial angeordneten Tierhöfen um einen zentralen Pavillon errichten. In diesem wird das Kaiserehepaar ab und zu frühstücken. Bestückt wird die neue Menagerie mit Beständen aus der des Belvederes. Ankäufe, Schenkungen und Expeditionen bringen Exoten nach Wien. 1779 wird der Tiergarten für das Volk geöffnet, im Laufe des 19. Jahrhunderts werden Gehege umgebaut, andere neu errichtet. Elefanten und Kamele erregen Aufsehen, seit 1828 aber insbesondere eine Giraffe. Sie beeinflusst sogar die Mode – Accessoires und Coiffuren „à la Giraffe" sind in. Am Ende des 19. Jahrhunderts erhält die Menagerie ein neues Gesicht, nämlich das eines zoologischen Gartens. Die Mauern werden durch Gitter ersetzt, um „Schaustücke besser in Augenschein zu nehmen". In den 1990er-Jahren werden die Gehege runderneuert und auf den modernsten Stand der Tierhaltung gebracht, ohne jedoch dem Tiergarten seinen historischen Charme zu nehmen. Der Tiergarten Schönbrunn ist der wahrscheinlich älteste noch bestehende Zoo der Welt.

Franz I Stephan is not only interest in flora but also fauna, and so he calls on the architect Nicolas Jadot in 1751 to erect a zoo complex in the form of 13 animal pens arranged in a radial pattern around a central pavilion – where the imperial couple will take breakfast from time to time. The new zoo is filled with stock from the menagerie at Belvedere. Exotic animals arrive in Vienna by way of purchases, donations and expeditions. The zoo is opened to the public in 1779, and during the 19th century some of the pens are refurbished while new ones are built. Elephants and camels draw wide attention and, from 1828 on, even more so a giraffe. The animal even has an impact on fashion – accessories and hair designs "à la giraffe" are en vogue. The menagerie is remodelled at the end of the 19th century to become a zoological garden. The walls are replaced by bars to get a better view of the objects on display. The enclosures are thoroughly renovated in the 1990s to bring them up to the most recent standards in animal care, yet without robbing the zoo of its historic charm. The Schönbrunn Zoo is probably the oldest zoo in the world still in existence.

Tiergarten Schönbrunn / Schönbrunn – the zoo

Impressum
Imprint

Konzept: Peter Hammermüller
Bildredaktion: Marlene Schönwetter
Text: Alexandra Binder
Grafik und Layout: Martina Gaigg

Idea: Peter Hammermüller
Picture editing: Marlene Schönwetter
Text: Alexandra Binder
Graphic design and layout: Martina Gaigg

Ferrytells Verlags- und BeratungsgmbH

Bildnachweise
Picture credits